INTERNALIZE

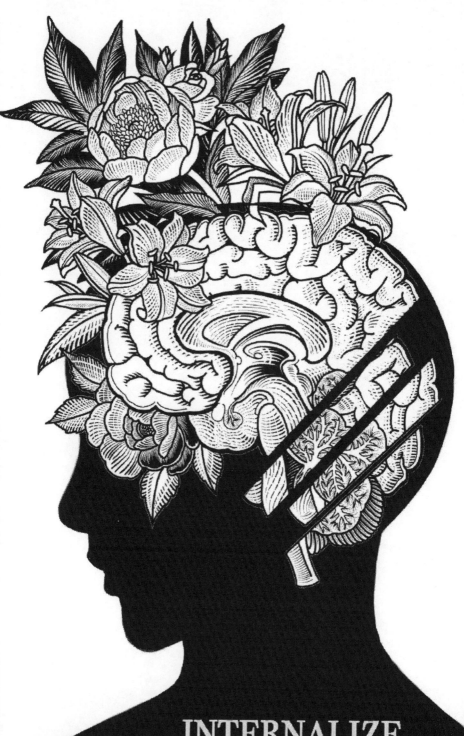

INTERNALIZE

J.A. Handville

First U.S. paperback edition 2018

Editing: Valerie Marie Valentine
Formatting: Joshua A. Handville
Design & Illustrations: Jamie Santos
@jamiesantosart

Manufactured in the United States of America

ISBN: 978-1717400024

To Allie and Parker:

With your guiding light,
I continue to forge a path through
my internal darkness and despair,
knowing that somewhere
deep within myself
lies the budding fruit
of my happiness,
a depraved emotion
I thought I no longer possessed.

I have the hope and strength to try
to reach out and inspire
other broken and desperate souls,
like myself,
through your unconditional love.

And I could never
thank you enough.

This book is dedicated
to each of you.

What a writer truly grants the reader
is the opportunity to glimpse into their soul.
Every word is a piece of them,
meticulously crafted with the utmost care.
The reader should never take for granted
this unguarded vulnerability.

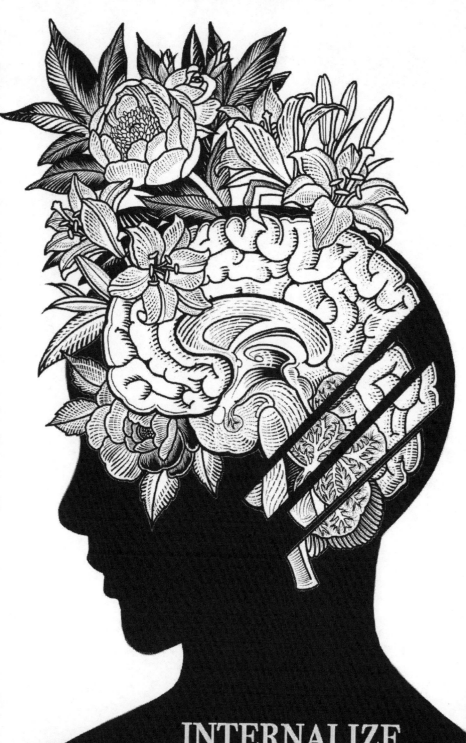

INTERNALIZE

J.A. HANDVILLE

Perhaps if a writer tears out
enough shards of their soul
and carefully hides them
in clever places,
they'll break the constraints
of mortality,
and never face the permanence
of death.

Author's Note

I've always believed that some of the most magnificent works of art stem from transforming internal chaos and pain into something undeniably beautiful. A broken individual finding the strength to mold their suffering into not only a tangible creation, but one that can touch the hearts of those consuming it has always reinforced my appreciation for artists and their craft. Some of the most influential lyrics, poems, and paintings I've ever had the pleasure of absorbing were handcrafted manifestations of the artist's own internal turmoil and despair.

It must be stated, dear readers, that this book of poetry comes from a source of pain and suffering as well— one that has been delicately shaped into a heart-filled creation designed to inspire those who identify themselves as broken.

There's a distinct purpose behind why I chose the name *Internalize* to represent the collection of poetry you'll find gently tucked away within these pages. The word "internalize," in itself, has a dual meaning; one is used far more frequently than the other, but each is equally significant to the framework of this book. The lesser used meaning refers to concealing your emotions and feelings instead of expressing them, while the other means to accept ideas, beliefs, or behaviors and make them an integral part of who you are.

The structure of this book is separated into two different parts, which not only replicate the dual meaning of the book's title, but also demonstrates how I perceive my own divided mind. These parts are The Broken Hemisphere and The Hopeful Hemisphere.

The Broken Hemisphere contains introspective pieces focused on anxiety, depression, heartbreak, and the multitude of other negative emotions associated with them. The Broken Hemisphere serves as a means through which to unveil the emotions and thoughts I internalize, the things I try to hide beneath my skin. By revealing them to you, I strive to not only make myself vulnerable and relate to you, but also prove that you are not alone in the burdens that you bear. Others feel pain like yours as well.

The Hopeful Hemisphere consists of uplifting and empowering messages specifically designed to inspire you during your darkest days. With compassionate poetry, I seek not only to demonstrate my own moments of triumph, but to help guide you to yours as well. These are the particular pieces I hope you internalize and mold into the divine structure of your being.

Countless artists have contributed to my continued existence through their selfless devotion to their work. Their words, their music, their paintings were the only thing penetrating the enveloping fog of darkness that engulfed me on the days I couldn't fight for myself. And I could never thank them enough for their creations.

I can only hope that my own contribution to the ever-expanding world of artistry is equally impactful to others. Who knows, perhaps my words might just break through to you.

It's that much, and that much alone, that I can only hope for.

— J.A. Handville

Contents

The Broken Hemisphere

The Hopeful Hemisphere

INTERNALIZE

THE BROKEN
HEMISPHERE

A Mind of Emptiness

Hollow out my emotions without mercy.
Silence my thoughts in their entirety.
Leave behind the skeletal remains of my memory.

I would rather possess a mind of emptiness
than one of unprovoked madness.

Hemispheres Unknown

With pure determination,
gaze into the inner workings of my mind,
where mental shards drift freely,
where once-aligned pathways unbind.

An emotional disturbance,
one that takes eons to subside,
has made its presence a continuous occurrence.
It methodically destroys me from the inside.

With my mental distress described to you,
man of remedy and cure,
urgently begin my mind's procedure.
Remove from me what I cannot endure.

I beg you, surgeon of unrivaled skill,
please silence all these desperate tears.
Cut out this emotional ebb and flow
I've disguised beneath my flesh for years.

I'm numb without a need for anesthesia,
surgeon of immaculate precision,
so please isolate each section of my past
with the graceful touch of each incision.

Take the scalpel and with the steadiest hands,
divide my brain into hemispheres unknown.
Sever away the memories inside
of a time I'll never know.

Peacefulness, companionship,
joy, love, and hope.
Cut away all wishful thinking
for this mind has lost its will to cope.

<u>Parasite of the Mind</u>

Residing within the vast depths of a deteriorating mind, hungrily devouring unsuspecting thoughts and emotions, lies a gluttonous parasite. Selfish by nature, its sole objective revolves around the systematic depletion of its host's positive mentality. Only through the extinction of hope and happiness does this parasite obtain what it desires most: absolute control over its host.

As the determined parasite begins its life's purpose, it understands almost immediately that overpowering the immensely complex mind of its host is a gradual process, one that cannot be taken lightly. It advances cautiously into its subject's fragile subconscious fibers, latching itself in secret and evading the illuminating spotlight of the host's consciousness through quick and cunning maneuvers.

Adaption, the parasite knows, is vital to its survival. It carefully calculates and accounts for the varying emotional states and thought processes its host cycles through and reacts accordingly. Obtaining this knowledge is of grave importance to the parasite, for only through the manipulation of the host's emotional triggers can it truly thrive without restraint.

Discovering the coordinates to prominent sources of positive thoughts and emotions, this heartless parasite begins to methodically destroy the unprotected mind of its host. Its exceptional ability to rapidly corrupt these once-positive energy sources and harness their negative by-product serves as the root cause of this parasite's increasing strength. Once the mind of the host is significantly weakened, there's no stopping the destructive nature of this persistent parasite.

Siphoned of nearly all positive energy sources, the host begins to experience an undeniable perspective change towards their outlook on life. An unparalleled darkness sweeps through even the deepest corners of the host's mind, blanketing hopeful aspirations and gentle dreams with a dense, suffocating smoke. Desperately drying and cracking beneath the strain, the parasite witnesses the delicate ambitions of its host crumble in catastrophic fashion. Beneath the rubble, hopelessness sets in.

The parasite is finally satisfied with its newfound home.

Questioning the sudden emptiness and despair, the conscious mind of the host eventually illuminates the source of this drastic mentality alteration. Beneath the all-seeing gaze of consciousness, the vicious parasite knows it can no longer hide—but it no longer needs to. For even after its inevitable destruction, its presence will be forever felt in the host's emotional triggers until yet another new and equally determined candidate is born.

This systematic cycle is seemingly unending. It's an everlasting illness devoid of the comforts of a remedy, a sense of despair and hopelessness from within that's immeasurable by any known human instrument, a perpetual darkness without a shred of illumination.

I call this the parasite of the mind.

Alone

Loneliness

in life went far enough
back for me.

Now I'm willing to stop looking
for answers to loneliness.

My loneliness is a given
and always has been.

It represents
a way of seeing
life.

I believe that everyone
born has a purpose
in life's vision,

and I am
the only creature
not born in harmony
with life.

<u>An Echo No Longer Heard</u>

The misery,   it grew.

Its presence became   so obvious.

Unfaltering   hope was

a darkening shadow,   an echo which lingered,

cautiously surviving between moments.

Suddenly, there was an internal scream—

My hope had disappeared.

General Misconception

People have a general misconception
that those suffering from depression
perceive suicide as the end of their life.

But that isn't the case at all.

You see,
people suffering from depression
have already perceived themselves as dead
for quite some time.

To them,
suicide is just a means by which
to dispose of the corpse.

Inkwell of Heartache

Introduction

As piercing gusts of freezing winds
howl against withered trees within
a frost-plagued forest utterly devoid
of any nocturnal noise,

my irrepressible sorrow drifts to silence
as I acknowledge, with soul-crushing compliance,
your heartbreaking words and the absence
of your warm and gentle voice.

Now left as a heartbroken and desperate man,
I humiliatingly beg and plead when I can
for one last, sincere opportunity
to win back your heart.

But alas, the hands of fate are working against us
as our love's restoration is never discussed,
and I'm painfully forced to witness
the death of us.

For on this night,

you wrote a tragic end
to our beautiful tale,
a conclusion defined
by heartbreak and sorrow.
You scribbled out the parts
in which our love prevails
beneath the gentle rays
of a brighter tomorrow.

Isolated by winter's harsh bitterness,

peering into this luminous wilderness,
I pointlessly search for answers
engraved in the snow.

Endless questions still flood my mind
despite explanations of every kind
that escaped from the lips of a woman
I once knew.

You blamed our countless differences,
my depression and self-destructiveness,
and the way I left my hopes and dreams
behind.

Yet beneath the struggles of my internal war,
I still loved you more than ever before
all I needed was a moment of clarity
and a little more time.

Instead,

you wrote a tragic end
to our beautiful tale,
a conclusion defined
by heartbreak and sorrow.
You scribbled out the parts
in which our love prevails
beneath the gentle rays
of a brighter tomorrow.

Now there's a cold emptiness,
an unpleasant, depressive ambience,
to this hollow shell of a place
we once called home.

Where our memories are shattered remnants

INTERNALIZE

of youthful love and innocence,
where your presence can still be felt
within these walls.

Yet beneath this moonlit winter night,
my weary self begins to write
poetic verses that express
this concealed pain.

Still the coldness of your words
can never simply be unheard
they relentlessly haunt
the darkest corners of
my mind.

"I don't love you anymore."
"I don't love you anymore."
"I don't love you ..."
"I don't ..."

Part I

Your disheartening
words of certainty
transformed my heart
into pure blackness;
a thick liquid
of the darkest sort
and the unwanted source
of my madness.

<u>Part II</u>

Through waves of doubt,
I've dipped my quill
into this inkwell
of heartache
to write words
that divert my pain
and create verses
that hopefully restrain
the flood of misery
flowing through my veins.

Part III

I desperately try
to empty this sorrow
from the polluted core
of my being.

And search the remains
of my hollow heart
to create a life
with renewed meaning.

Yet memories of you
watermark these new pages
of a future I desire to write.

And your relentless presence
consumes my present
and destroys my state of mind.

<u>Echoes of Her</u>

The sound of her movement
growing fainter
through the room had changed
his mind.

He waited,
and the sounds continued
to diminish.

He could hear them still:
sounds,
unplaceable echoes.

After several minutes,
the flame began to shrink.

It went out,
shrank to the charring end.

He stood for a moment,
cringing from the coldness.

He cringed back
instinctively
against the flood of emotion.

<u>Endure</u>

Repeatedly,
I have felt the fibers of my own soul being torn apart.
Day after day, night after night.
It's so repetitious, so predictable.
Yet I never seem to get used to the feeling.
It's as if I'm suffering a thousand deaths before I die.
And I must **endure the pain** of each one.

This Hard Place of Weakness and Silence

He feared it,
this hard place of weakness and silence.

She was like all the others
that haunted him
these days.

The light died.

The shadows grew deeper.

His eyes upon hers
help him understand
his way back to life.

He regretted his necessity
and
dropped away to sleep.

The Meaning of the Dream

What was born in me
with certainty
came from
the silence of my heart.

> Love,
> upon which,
> moved me
> as I sank to my knees.

> I recognized her without
> the slightest difficulty.

> There was an ethereal beauty about her.
> The light seemed to come from her,
> communicated to her,
> fully visible to me.

My mind
had this reassuring dream,
the memory of it
as delightful as ever.

> Her loving smile;
> I can still feel the touch of
> the kisses she gave me. And now,
> this tenderness

> means to leave me.

INTERNALIZE

Will you come and fetch me soon?

I promise you, more of me.

<u>Sleep Deprived</u>

Restlessly,

        my weary eyes

cast their sight

        to the illumination

of the moonlight.

        As exhausted whimpers

escape

        their internal captivity,

my release of

        self-perceived weakness

begins, yet again,

        within the darkness

of another sleepless

        night.

Torn Between Her and I

To still be madly in love
with a person
who no longer exists
in the same way that's been
ingrained,
embedded,
and burned
into the internal tunnels
of your malleable brain
is perhaps the most intense pain
one can ever feel.

When the stranger you know
is still living,
but the person you once knew
is dead,
and both of those people
are one in the same,
it haunts you in ways
I cannot possibly describe.

The memories come in floods,
and you can't help but obsessively
dwell on the past,
peering desperately into old photographs,
and wishing every second spent
during those time-forgotten moments
would have lasted
a lifetime.

And it kills me ...

It kills me
to try to erase her

The Broken Hemisphere

from my thoughts
as if
she meant nothing at all
to me.

And it kills me
to continue preserving
these beautiful memories
of her
while my own sanity
crumbles into dust.

I'm torn between
losing myself
and losing her
within the confines of
my own chaotic mind ...

and I've already lost her
once before.

Manifestation

In a past I now mourn, she was my perception of life's beauty. I peered through her like a kaleidoscope, staring in wonder as her enthusiasm and happiness created an endless variety of bliss-inducing patterns. The images of life she effortlessly reflected were enticing, mesmerizing even. I kept peering through her until she became my only source for experiencing the magnificence of life. She became my addiction, and I became an addict. She became a host for my happiness, and I became the parasite.

It was this emotional dependency that drove us apart.

In the aftermath of all this, I believe my depression assumed a new form. I believe it sought out that which had the tendency to expose my deepest weaknesses and shaped itself into an immaculate recreation of it. Something designed to haunt my recovering mind.

I believe my depression manifested itself as her.

She is the perfect disguise for my mind-devouring mental torment. My depression knows how powerful her presence is within me, so its vile claws have latched on and corrupted it. This darkness has infected the memories I once held so dear. It has siphoned out the happiness from each one, leaving the dried remains to decompose within my tortured mind. And worse yet, it forces me to continuously witness this defilement of our past relationship.

My depression's demoralizing imitation of her lingers within the farthest reaches of my peripheral vision, and all I can do is silently watch it destroy me.

This idea is cultivating me, shaping me into something entirely different. If I wish to survive, I must control what seeks to control me. I must mold something

positive out of this overwhelming source of negativity.
Or I fear I'll become lost forever.

<u>What Lies in the Silence</u>

There are no words
in any language
of mankind's creation
that can effectively
and wholly describe
true love or
true pain.

For to truly experience them
is to acknowledge the silence
that both will bring.

That silence
makes the intensity
of either emotion
appear.

Silence.

It's that noun
that describes what
true love and
true pain
is like
far better than
any adjective
ever could.

For to experience
true love,
you must embrace
the silence.

You must embrace it

with every fiber
of your being.

You must embrace silence
for it allows
the steady,
rapid beating
of your devoted
lover's heart
to resonant within your ears,
lingering there,
willingly,
like a favorite song
you wish to hear.

You must embrace silence
for it allows
the soft,
soothing sound
of a tender kiss
upon your forehead
to feel that much more
endearing.

You must embrace silence
for it allows
the gentle warmth
of the person
you're embracing
to speak softly
to you,

communicating words
of silent compassion
aimed directly
at you.

INTERNALIZE

I know,
deep down,
you recognize
that all of this
is true.

For if you listen clearly
to your thoughts
swirling in and out of
your consciousness,
you'll know that
every memory of love
that you cling to,
like your life
depends on it,
starts within
the confines of
the silence.

And that can be said
when we are faced with
true pain.

But that silence
yields a different meaning
to each of us.

You must bear silence
as the pain allows
the sensation of
internalized fear
to destroy every
positive thought
you so desperately
need to hear.

The Broken Hemisphere

You must bear silence
as the pain allows
the dark flow of
deceiving depression
to jeopardize everything
you hold so dear
as you obsessively dwell
on what continues to
suspend you
in sadness
and fear.

You must bear silence
as the pain allows
each tear of pure
and utter misery
to drop silently
without time to create
a proper eulogy,
despite the significance
of each one of those tears.

And how much each tear
truly means
to you.

I know,
deep down,
you recognize
that all of this
is true.

For if you listen clearly
to your thoughts
swirling in and out of
your consciousness,

INTERNALIZE

you'll know that
every memory of pain
that you wish
to rid yourself of
starts within
the confines of
the silence.

Silence.

I never thought
a single word could be
so drastically changed
simply by
the emotion
put behind it.

A World Away

The memories
were fading.

Hope had
completely decayed.

The rest of life
took place
a world away
and
ended in a flood of words.

Letters held messages.

There appeared to be
poems in the pauses.

And the night
forbid him
to go.

Nail Biter

Determined teeth
gnaw away
with machine-like
efficiency
at stubborn cuticles
and innocent fingernails.

As they are left
to bleed again
beneath my relentless
onslaught,
I begin to question
why I have deemed this
an appropriate method
of coping with
the uncertainty
surrounding
my forthcoming
and unforeseeable future.

Introspectively,
I persistently shovel
the false information,
the shifting perspectives,
and the endless lies
out of the vast depths
of my malleable mind,

but I'm already

well aware

of what lies here.

The Broken Hemisphere

Hesitantly,
I reveal
blackened roots
secured by fear
entangling the images
of a future I've envisioned
for myself
in a time
when uncertainty didn't
envelop my mind.

And this particular truth,
I must admit to myself.

And this particular truth,
I must permanently uproot.

What I truly fear
is uncertainty,
and since
the entirety
of this thing called life
is governed by
uncertainty,
I guess,
in the grand scheme of things,
I fear life,
and essentially,
that also means
I fear
what it truly means
to live,
which is strange,
in a sense,
because all I crave
out of life

INTERNALIZE

is to feel as if

I'm truly alive.

Thus,
this cycle
of anxiety
continues.

Anxiety continues.
Anxiety continues.
Anxiety continues.
Anxiety continues
eternally.

So I bite,
crunch,
tear,
and rip
these fingernails
apart.

I reshape them,
no matter how imperfectly.

It's the shape of them,
and perhaps this alone,
that I know I can
occasionally control.

Bound

My mind

had been bound

by the past.

I had no awareness of time.

I was to remain

here

with guilt

in my life.

That worried me.

Memento Mori

Beneath the crushing sands of time,
an illusion perceived by all mankind,
lies the distressed mentality of a man
fighting for a life that's barely began.

Paranoid that his brief time on Earth
will be as meaningless as he perceives his worth,
he allows the persistence of the sands
to engulf his mind and delay life's plans.

Hindered by a treacherous distortion of truth.
Haunted by the withering of his youth.
He acknowledges the absence of his dreams.
An internal voice becomes one desperate scream.

Left to confront anxiety beyond his own comprehension,
the lingering presence of depression increases the tension.
A pressure, a weight beyond what his mind can withstand.
So he drifts even further beneath the sand.

Each precious grain represents the present slipping by.
Yet his deceiving thoughts shackle him to the lie
that he will do nothing of meaning with his life,
that his mind will never witness a moment without strife.

Beneath the crushing sands of time,
an illusion perceived by all mankind,
lies the distressed mentality of a man
dying before his life even began.

<u>Life Machine</u>

With burning curiosity,
I've gazed deeply into the hollow eyes
of the lost and soulless wanderers.
And though my compassion
for these poor and lonely individuals
has never once wavered,
there was once a time
where I did not understand
what could ever cause someone
to willingly become
a hopeless shell of a human being.

I would question
their cold, robotic sensibilities,
even as I acknowledged
the mechanical hum
of their hearts beating.

I would question
their depressing, repetitious nature
to dissolve life as quickly as possible,
even as I witnessed
their weary and weakened minds
fall victim to the infectious virus
of purposelessness
and materialistic delusion.

And I would question
their transparent disinterest
in molding anything substantial
and unquestionably meaningful
out of the beautifully constructed concept
of their own existence,
even as I felt

INTERNALIZE

their frail and desperate souls
be gradually gnawed away at
by the insatiable and selfish mouth
of existential death.

Yet, I must admit to myself
that I did not truly understand
the knowledge brought forth
by these perceptive observations
until the moment arrived
when I suddenly transformed
into a life machine

like them.

Now I understand
what it's like to die
within a mind and body
that's still living.

Extinction of Identity

Swirling distortions
and inconsistent shapes
replace once distinguished
facial lines.

Colors bleed and blend
as my form escapes
from the image of
my blurry reflection.

Vision still shifting,
I concentrate harder
but my focus is shattered
beyond reasonable repair.

There's no resemblance
of human form present here
as I helplessly gaze
into this mirror of despair.

What my mind now perceives
is merely an illusion of me,
a composition devoid
of its natural distinction.

My identity is now forced
to unwillingly acknowledge
the overwhelming sensation
of its gradual extinction.

Existential Death

I was critically ill
with no feeling except
a mild curiosity.

I seemed to sense
I was simply

dying.

People who are close to dying
almost never feel pain.

I had no interest in
a feeling of peace,
a sense that all was well.

I lapsed into a timeless blank

without any sense
that I possessed

a body.

The Brink of Insanity

Disappear within your endless tears of self-pity.

Collapse beneath the weight of your worthlessness.

The beauty of life was wasted on you.

Your existence is devoid of meaning, and it will never possess any sense of purpose.

You will wander aimlessly and hopelessly until your inevitable end arrives.

Loneliness will forever be your only true companion.

Misery will extinguish the flicker of hope you hold so dear.

You will become a prisoner in your own mind and stripped of your sanity.

Love has eluded you, for you cannot be loved.

You are alone in this world, and even your own mind has betrayed you.

You will never heal from the scars your heart has suffered.

No one will remember you when you're gone.

No one will remember you when you're gone.

No one will remember you when you're gone.

Waste your time pursing your dreams, you will never accomplish what you seek.

You will know perpetual darkness, and you will become one with it.

You will be relentlessly tormented by a past you cannot change.

The memories you cling to will experience corruption beyond your comprehension.

No one will understand your pain, and your words will fall on deaf ears.

You will witness time age you into dust as you silently suffer.

Tangle yourself within the webs of self-doubt, for all you can ever hope to achieve is failure.

You seek to cheat your own mortality, yet your life isn't even worth remembering.

INTERNALIZE

Those who have left you behind knew you were a waste of time.

The voice you've tried so desperately to silence is your only source of truth and reason.

You will break beneath the endless onslaught of your own deceiving thoughts.

You will know the true meaning of pain and suffering.

I will always be a part of you, lingering internally within the deepest confines of your mind.

You will never rid yourself of my presence.

You will never rid yourself of my presence.

...when will this internal voice end its painful repetition?

__Rip Myself Apart__

Realign the threads of fabric
that contain who I am.
Carefully, carelessly,
with precision or not.

I care not.
I care not.
I care not.

Tear apart these threads of memory.
Alter the strands that make me "Me."
For this discouraging life of mine
will never quite properly define
who I truly am
and who I truly am not
with an accurate and clear definition.

And that is what I seek.

My own indecision
towards the life that I've been living,
so cautiously or carelessly,
with endless pain consuming me,
is relentlessly haunting me.

My own indecision
is simply
killing me.

I'm dying without
death overtaking me.

I'm heartless with
a heart that's still beating.

INTERNALIZE

I'm breathless with
lungs that are still breathing.

And I believe
it's finally time for me
to rip myself apart
and see what lies
beneath.

I must rip myself apart.
Rip myself apart.
Rip myself apart.

Rip.
Myself.
Apart.

I must
because I know,
I hope,
there just simply
must be

something better
that is seeking to be
discovered
deep within me.

This is my renewal ...

But first,
I must rip myself apart.

<u>Deaf Planet</u>

"Listen to me,
please listen to me,
you tragically confused
creatures."

Outside the deafening roar
of a restless planet,
a lonely Universe speaks
to an inattentive audience
of unnecessarily noisy
and inconsiderate speakers
aimlessly wandering through
the duration of their existence.

These decaying minds spew
relentless negativity.
These empty vessels ignore
their self-loathing tendencies.
And these dying souls shout
filthy vulgarities
at what is perceived to be
a cruel and hopeless world.

But a determined Universe
tries once again
to project her voice
and engrave her words
into the soft tissue
of each sad,
troubled, and withering mind.

"Listen to me,
please listen to me,
you tragically confused

creatures.

If only you opened
yourselves up to me,
things would appear,
I promise they'd appear,
much differently
than they currently seem. "

Yet through the vocal dissonance,
no one hears the nurturing words
of the Universe's desperate
and sorrowful pleads.

Gentle cries that beg
the human race to see
the misconception
in their beliefs
and the error
in their ways.

<u>Our Void</u>

Deep within
the farthest reaches of
our being
lies a repressed sense
of emptiness,
one whose roots
are secured permanently
into the core
of our existence.

This lingering feeling
is a seemingly
everlasting
source of hollowness
whose hunger is
impossible
to satisfy.

It is the result of
the rips and tears
our hearts and souls
endure,
despite
our desperate attempts
to self-mend.

And tragically,
we have grown
to know this
manifestation
within us
quite well.

This opposition to

INTERNALIZE

our contentment,
the very fuel
that sustains
our feeling of
incompleteness,

is called our void.

The Mask of the Masses

In the presence of life,
I have found that often
people are wearing

a mask
to conceal
deep doubts

to cope with
the problems of
living.

The Hurt Ones

I've come to acknowledge
that many of the same people
that experience unbearable
pain and suffering
are also the first ones
to listen and help others
through their pain.

They know firsthand
what it's like to endure
the brokenness of heartache,
the emptiness of existential death,
the hopelessness of depression,
and the helplessness of anxiety.

They are the ones
that truly care
and understand
what you are going through.

Believe me when I say
that they are also the ones
. who would siphon
the pain,
the misery,
the sorrow,
and the suffering
straight out of you
and place it deep
within themselves
if they were ever given
the chance.

They are the ones

who would bear
your despair
for you.

For to them,
words feel as if
they are barely enough
to help others through
their devastating circumstances.

They feel
the desperation of others,
the pain of others,
the suffering of others,
and they make it
their own mission
to help others
rid these toxic feelings
out of themselves.

They form meaningful words
into illuminating sentences
that pierce through the darkened state
of these poor individuals.

They are The Hurt Ones,
the ones fiercely battling
the all-consuming infernos
of their own internalized hell.

Yet,
they still postpone
the unseen inner conflict
raging on within themselves
to ensure that others
do not hurt as much

as they do.

They are the ones who fight
the darkness for others
while their own darkness slowly
consumes them.

They are the ones who fuel
hollowed-out hearts with hope
while their own hearts ache
with unresolved despair.

They are the ones who heal
the broken,
scarred,
and wounded structures
of other souls
while their own souls tragically
crumble into ruin.

They are
The Hurt Ones,

and they will always
seek out to heal you
before they ever manage
to heal themselves.

Darkness & Light

To dwell in the darkness
is to experience
conflicting suffering.

You encounter
the misery that plagues you,
that much is certain.

Yet you also develop
a deeper appreciation
for the light.

It becomes a brief respite.

A moment of internal peace.

A sense of hope within a raging
and perceivably everlasting storm.

And without that initial despair,
perhaps we wouldn't treasure
these instances as intensely
as we do.

Darkness cannot exist without light.

And light cannot exist without darkness.

Neither can be recognized without
the presence of the other.

Please, remember that.

INTERNALIZE

Remember these words
when you're weeping in despair.

Remember these words
when you're silently suffering.

Remember these words
when your misery seems
too much for you to bear.

It is through conquering our darkest moments
that we learn how to fully embrace
the intensity of the light.

THE HOPEFUL
HEMISPHERE

Promise

I'm here to tell you
that I've experienced
what giving up
feels like,

and I promise you

you're far better
and far stronger
than your despair.

Compassion

I hope,
with every ounce of compassion
my heart holds,
that you will find words
within these pages
that impact
your soul.

For perhaps,
through you,
I can also begin
to mend
myself.

<u>Diminishing the Fever</u>

He had to

       diminish

              the fever

in his own mind.

Hope's Arrival

The fever began
                    and he slept more.

            Hope
            watched every moment
            with her patient eyes,
            beneath the luminous
            moonlight.

He grew restless,
                        tossing again.

                            She spoke his name.

                    He stopped his restless movements

and seemed to listen.

            She thoughtfully
            began to speak again,
            sitting down a little way
            from the bed,
            softly, quietly, as one would read
            to soothe a child.

    "Let not your heart be troubled.

            Believe in me."

Dead Words

The faintness of deception's whisper
resonates deeply within my mind.
Consciously, I acknowledge these questions
proposed by an internal demon I cannot bind.

What is the purpose of your existence?
Can you even define your life's meaning?
Or are you compelled to keep wandering this Earth
until the moment of death's intervening?

Pondering over these disheartening questions,
I feel the demon's blackened corruption spread.
First it extinguishes the hope in my heart,
before viciously overpowering the thoughts in my head.

I helplessly scream out for mercy,
but even my most desperate cries are silenced.
Words wither and die before they escape my lips,
a victim to cold and calculated compliance.

My inner self writhes in agony,
powerless to the whims of this malevolent foe.

I am your mind's darkness manifested,
a void of infinite woe.

This evil's assertive words endlessly echo.
They pierce through the fabric of my soul.
But just when all internal peace seems lost,
I feel myself gain momentary control.

A gasp of breath expands my lungs
as newfound strength reshapes my being.
The courage to resist pulses through these veins.
Through misery itself, I shall claim my life's meaning.

INTERNALIZE

Wretchedness personified,
you infectious plague of darkness,

I acknowledge I've been granted free will
devoid of any purpose.

Cruel deception,
don't you remember?
You've imprisoned my mind before.

Through your countless lies,
this cycle survives—
we're rivals in a waging war.

These empowering words reverberate
deep within my consciousness.
An internal rejuvenation stems
from pure and utter hopelessness.

My voice of reason,
toned with conviction,
will never become a casualty.

For this demon may still have a hold on me,

but I'll never succumb to its false sense of reality.

Exist

Sometimes I live for myself,
sometimes I live for others.
Each are of equal importance to me.
Each give my existence substance and meaning.

The times I live for myself,
I practice the words I preach.
I attempt to be an ear for the broken
and a voice for the lost.

The times I live for others,
I ensure that my voice resonates with strength
and my words **don't become empty and hollow.**

The moments where you're at your worst,
when **others are counting on you** the most,
are when **your existence means more** to them
than you'll ever know.

You never know when
you are the source of someone's hope.

The Truth About Suicide

The overbearing pain,
the burdensome negative energy
that's concealed beneath your flesh
and pumping through your veins,
does not disperse
once your existence
has met its self-initiated demise.

It grows.

It unleashes itself
and reveals its full potential,
in the wake of your absence,
by mercilessly consuming
all those that love
and care about you.

And I know your purpose isn't
to hurt the ones you love.

This isn't an elaborate method
through which to make you feel guilty
about storing away depressing thoughts
pertaining to the end of your existence.

This is one compassionate
and understanding heart
trying to communicate,
so desperately,
to your broken soul.

The Hopeful Hemisphere

I believe that you are stronger than
the demons that consume you.

I beg you,
please do not become
just another statistic.

Internal War

We may find ourselves
trapped beneath
the crushing hands of
despair,
weak
and desperate,
but we must seek
the strength within ourselves
to press on.

If that reservoir has
run empty,
if every fiber of
our being
has been greatly compromised,
we must seek out
a source of strength
in others.

Although we fight
tooth and nail
in the internal battles
that plague us,
lonely
and drifting
towards hopelessness,
this waging war
is not ours alone
to fight.

We cannot surrender to
the dying light,
the perpetual darkness
that devours
our precious minds.

The Hopeful Hemisphere

We cannot be
yet another victim
of this deceiving void.

This is a war for our minds.

A war over
the very essence of who we are.

And with that knowledge,
we must emerge
victorious.

Inevitable Relief

When your reservoir of hope
is severely depleted,
and you feel helpless
beneath the crushing weight
of your pain,
please
try to remember
that even the heaviest downpours
must make way
for the sunlight's
inevitable appearance.

Perspective Change

~~He looked back and recalled old conversations.~~
It hurt him that he harbored thoughts of her.

He tried ~~to get away from it all.~~
to leave her free to go her way.

Once, he went after her, afterward
~~wondering why she wished to leave.~~
to give her love and admiration.

And when she set herself
to the winds,
in the face of everything,
~~he lost her.~~
he grew.

He hunted out
the beauty in life.

With this perspective,
he was

                                    set free.

Dying Embers

With gentle hands,
I delicately sift through
the smoldering ashes
of this beautiful inferno
we once called love.

As the darkened debris
disguises my flesh
with black residue,
I painfully remember
the mesmerizing flames
of what we once were.

It's this particular memory
that's burned permanently
into the tissue-dense center
of my tormented mind.

Barely repressing
the emotional cycling
and overthinking tendencies
of this captivating pain
called heartache,
I continue to scour
through the poignant remains
of our long-extinguished,
but once-passionate fire,

an eternal fire

that burned out
too soon.

From the dying embers
of this

unceremoniously
smoldering abyss,

I seek only that
which is mine:

the missing fragments,
the abandoned,
shattered segments,
of my once intact
identity.

So I diligently dust off
the soot engulfing
each carefully collected
transparent shard,

and precisely realign
each precious piece
of my scorched
and scattered
identity.

Though this process
is delicate and timely,
each valued shard
rekindles peace from within.

A reconnection to what
was once missing before

sparks new hope
deep beneath my skin.

Mending the Fragments

Studying the sinking feeling
felt in his heart,
he held fragments of life
and happiness in his hands.

Only he possessed the hand
that could put them together again
if they were ever to go on.

In that defining moment,
his heart was lifted.

<u>Life Desires</u>

Inspiration,
may you fuel
my hungry mind
and fill
my hollow heart.

Imagination,
may you create
what mundane reality
cannot.

Motivation,
may you balance out
my numerous doubts
and allow me
to fulfill my dreams.

Modesty,
may you allow me
to remain humble
in the wake of
my success.

Knowledge,
may I never lose
the desire to
purse you
nor lose
the ability
to acquire you.

Happiness,
may I find comfort
in your warm embrace
without ever having

INTERNALIZE

to let you go.

Love,
may the inferno
of your divine passion
everlastingly engulf
the static fibers
of my heart and soul,
and never be
unceremoniously
extinguished.

Anxiety,
may the web of lies
you endlessly weave
dissolve beneath
the burning trifecta
of confidence,
experience,
and trust.

Depression,
may I conquer you
time and time again,
and never allow
your deceiving influence
to overpower
my mind.

Hope,
may I never lose
sight of you
in the aftermath
of loss and tragedy.

Life,
may these desires of mine

come to fruition
before my inevitable
time arrives.

Death,
may I forget
the countless times
my youthful self
almost sought out
comfort in your cold
and permanent presence
before I could appreciate
the beauty of life.

Sole Creator
(Dedicated to the Reader)

Do not let what you cannot control define you. You are the sole creator of your own destiny. Regardless of your past, you possess the capability to redefine how you view yourself.

For those suffering through unbearable mental distress or soul-crushing heartbreak, please know that your journey does not end where your misery began. Know that what you're experiencing now is not eternal. Know that your pain is not everlasting.

With everything you can muster, allow this misery to mold you into a stronger individual. Do not allow it to dissolve your confidence, dreams, or motivation. Do not allow it to smother your flame of hope.

We are meant to be hardened by our struggles, not destroyed by them. Rise from the smoldering wreckage of what you once were with a renewed state of mind. Only you possess the capability to overcome the intensity of your suffering and begin the process of your restructuring.

What I ask of you, dear sorrowful reader, is to become the embodiment of emotional strength. Begin to mend your broken soul with unwavering devotion. Carefully realign each fragmented shard with the knowledge that you're crafting a stronger version of yourself. And with patience and determination, your hope shall be restored.

Self-Worth

You are always worth more
than what you perceive.

Never devalue yourself
based on the false notion
that your existence
is meaningless
or that your life
is pointless.

The rise and fall
of your steady breathing
is worth far more
than these
conniving,
deceiving,
manipulative,
and self-loathing
thoughts.

Allow Me

*If sorrow is silencing
your tongue,*

*then allow me to be
your voice.*

*If tears are hurting
your will to write,*

*then allow me to be
your words.*

*And if the depths of
your suffering
are too much
for you to bear,*

*then allow me to be
your strength.*

The Hopeful Hemisphere

With my voice,
I will make sure
that your pain
doesn't go unheard
by the masses
you feel alone amongst.

With my words,
I will confess
the feelings
you repress,
and reveal to the world
my vulnerabilities
in hopes that one day
you will do the same.

And with my strength,
I will bear
the burden
of your misery
and reignite
the flame
in your heart.

For we may be
perfect strangers,
long-lost friends,
or distant neighbors,

but we all connect
in the sincerest fashion
through the understanding of
each other's pain.

Breathe New Life

People always replace
what they perceive is broken.

They replace things
to obtain something
that is new
to them.

Something that is
perceivably flawless
by design
to them.

Never truly knowing
the potential beneath
what they are thoughtlessly
leaving behind.

And I see that sentiment
so very clearly
within the dusty,
weathered confines
of this cramped
secondhand
bookstore.

A lifetime's worth
of battered books
aching for someone
to turn their pages

and breathe new life
into their warped spines.

The Hopeful Hemisphere

People always replace
what they perceive is broken.

But I will always
be there to
breathe new life
into you.

Reborn

I believe we die
a thousand times
in our lifetime.

And I believe
each death allows us
to be reborn.

But only we decide
how each one of those
deaths
shape us.

We can be reborn
as remarkably determined
and hopeful visionaries,

constructed
by the pillars
of immense inner strength,

engulfed
by the fires
of blazing motivation,

and illuminated
by the radiance
of enduring self-confidence.

Or,
in the most
depressing fashion,

we can be reborn
as irreversibly broken

and desperate souls,

consumed
by the tentacles
of our irrepressible past,

devoured
by the mouth
of our gluttonous guilt,

and crushed
by the shards
of our shattered aspirations.

No one ...

No one
makes it out of this life
the same way in which
they started.

We are the ones
who ultimately choose
what we will forever
become.

Perfect Imperfections

One of the worst things
we could possibly do
for ourselves
is search for perfection
in imperfect humans.

You will be disappointed
every time.

Our imperfections are
what make us unique.

They reflect

our personality,

our identity,

and our divine structure.

They are exactly
what make you
who you are.

I ask you,
dear readers,
to thrive
in your imperfections.

Not just for me,
but for yourselves as well.

The Hopeful Hemisphere

I ask this from you
because we are all imperfect.

And we are all perfectly fine
in our imperfections.

Pour Out (Self) Love

When we are open
with ourselves
and
g r o w,

our understanding
of ourselves
pours out love,

and helps us become
what we are capable
of becoming.

Karma & Kindness

It can be demoralizing
to be deemed weak
for consistently displaying
a sense of compassion
and humility

by those who perceive
cruelty
and selfishness
as ideal signs of strength,

but you must

push forward

with courage.

The depths
of your strong
and magnificent soul
must not succumb
to their close-minded
and dehumanizing delusions.

Remain ironclad in your belief
that treating others
with kindness and sympathy
will be reciprocated
in due time.

INTERNALIZE

I assure you,
karma's gentle
yet stern hand
will return your kindness
when you least expect it.

<u>Wisdom I</u>

You
possess the strength
to endure
what you believe
is impossible
to overcome.

Allow your heart
to strengthen
in the wake of
unbearable pain.

Allow your mind
to adapt
in the midst of
internal chaos.

And allow your soul
to illuminate
the darkness of
grief and sorrow.

These are all
the blooming buds of
beautiful wisdom.

<u>Wisdom II</u>

Wisdom
is enduring the burdens
and struggles of life,
but acknowledging
that there is still
beauty in it.

Natural Beauty

When one pursues
the inner peacefulness
and rejuvenating comfort
of solitude,
they are bound to uncover
its natural beauty.

This particularly
breathtaking beauty
gracefully develops
even within
the darkest corners
of the human mind,

if one allows it to.

So, focus.

Concentrate hard
and conceptualize
solitude's presence
within you.

First,
imagine
the swirling,
blooming buds
of purely satisfying
contentment,
which joyously
overwhelms the senses
and provides
unquestionable relief.

INTERNALIZE

Next,
visualize
the vibrant colors
and magnificent radiance
of fully blossomed
tranquility,
which gently
eases the mind
and cleanses
the accumulated toxins
of the soul.

Lastly,
envision
inhaling deeply
the intoxicating,
sense-stimulating
aroma
of *internal renewal,*
which lovingly encompasses
the flourishing atmosphere
of your freshly created
garden of solitude.

An exquisite garden
that you
and you alone
occupy.

Can you imagine it?

For within this imagery lies
a remarkable truth.

One that only solitude
can show us.

Life can be cold,
cruel,
and chaotic.

However,

life's true magnificence
will always be found
when we possess
a state of mind
where we can be
alone with ourselves
yet not be lonely.

That is where
a true appreciation
for life
always stems from.

And that
is the natural beauty
of solitude.

The Living Mountains

These mountains showed one's greatest fears.

They spoke of these cliffs,

"The Living Mountains."

Climb the cliffs alone.

Conquer   the mountains alone.

Look   down from the

heights to

the people below.

They
          never dared to   climb

and
f
e
l
l
into the abyss.

The courage to climb the mountains
brought about
the greatest wisdom

I have ever encountered.

Illumination of Purpose

What is the weight of our existence if we measure ourselves upon the scale of an infinite universe? Beneath the delusions we conceal ourselves behind, what is our true significance in the world? Imprisoned by the shackles of mortality, will our own contributions during our lifetime withstand the cruel and crushing nature of time? Or are we only destined to be forgotten, lost within the depths of a world that's forever evolving?

Perhaps these are the most significant questions one asks themselves when faced with the disheartening thoughts associated with an existential crisis. We question our purpose and the very concept of our own existence in search for a truth about ourselves that, we believe, we may never discover.

And what's heartbreaking is we readily accept this.

In pure desperation, we gaze up at star-filled night skies, admiring their glorious illumination while hopelessly questioning whether we will ever acquire such a vibrant radiance. One only acquires such radiance through the recognition of their life's purpose. It's at these particularly devastating moments where we feel the overbearing weight of the world. It's at these exact moments where we feel completely and utterly alone.

In the grand scheme of things, one's continued failure to discover their true purpose is not a fault entirely of their own. How can an individual possibly become aware of this incredible power within themselves without even the slightest indication of where to search?

To distract ourselves, we try to fill the bottomless void deep within us with questionable and unsubstantial things. Beneath the pulsation of our true destiny and undiscovered passions, we sacrifice our precious time to meaningless diversions that only hinder our progression in the end. Progression towards the very center of what makes us unique and gives our lives authentic and unquestionable purpose.

We are told that this is purely life's journey, that we all eventually find our purpose in the end. But is that actually true? So many seem to abandon their hopes and dreams that sometimes these words seem hollow, like they're used solely to comfort us during trying times. As a result, we develop the mindset that it's far easier to simply give up.

I'm here to say we cannot choose to dwell in hopelessness and accept failure as our only option.

We must remain hopeful in the fact that we can and will find our life's purpose, if, and only if, we continue to actively search for it with every fiber of our beings. As wanderers of the heart and soul, we must never stop searching for our own sense of purpose. It is perhaps the quintessential part of our existence. It's essential in determining who we are and, more importantly, who we will ultimately become.

Throughout our lives we will continue to gaze deeply into the vastness of the night sky, contemplating the nature of our existence and questioning what the grand significance of our life is. But we must never be intimidated by the radiance that the stars before us exhibit.

Reclaim your desire to find your definitive purpose and strive to maintain a positive mentality that allows you to thrive even in the face of failure. It's important to remember that we are never alone in this struggle to discover our purpose. We are all collectively seeking our calling in life, something that truly defines who we are to ourselves.

Always keep that in mind.

A Desired Discovery

What if

within all of us lies
a malleable
internal universe
that we ourselves possess
the mental strength
and capability
to mold?

What if

the true essence of
transcendence
lies within
the acceptance
that we can and will become
something more
than what we currently are?

The complexities
of our own emotions,
of our own anxieties,
of our own insecurities
might all eventually
become controllable
within the untapped
depths of our own minds.

What if

what we truly seek
lies buried within us
from the start,
awaiting its

INTERNALIZE

inevitable
discovery?

Perhaps
it's this concept of
transcending past
our current state of mind
that leads us to
tranquility
and everlasting
peace
within
ourselves.

It's this much,
and this much alone,
that I know I can only
hope for.

Remedy of the Heart & Mind

Never allow
the thoughts of the mind
to conquer
the emotions of the heart.

Repeatedly sacrificing
the soul's intuition
to sustain self-perceived
emotional strength
only fuels
internal destruction.

The perception of weakness,
defined as
an individual's desire
to unveil their emotions
and communicate
their vulnerabilities,
is false.

If we continue to harbor
that mentality,
it will only distort
our perspective of reality.

Consequently,
it will leave us with
an imitation of the life
we should be living.

We were never designed
to conceal
our emotional
and mental wounds.

INTERNALIZE

Heal through the hearts
of others.

Allow their words
of hope
to mend you.

And find strength
in the knowledge that
you are not alone.

This is the true remedy
of the heart and mind.

<u>Soul Creators</u>
(Dedicated to the Artists)

We are the patient artists
creating beauty out of pain
and happiness out of sorrow.

We are the vulnerable writers
forming verses with the torn pieces
of our hearts and souls.

We are the introspective musicians
peering deeply within ourselves
to create and connect to others
like us.

But most importantly,

we are the soul creators
rekindling the dying hope
of the mourners and sufferers.

As soul creators,
our true purpose
is to creatively
transform negative energy
into a positive outlet
of self-expression.

One that may help others
survive their own battle
with anxiety, heartbreak,
and crippling depression.

With unwavering hope,
we continue to prevail
in our fight to overcome

INTERNALIZE

what burdens us.

And our relentless dedication
shall continue to inspire
the broken, lonely,
and voiceless
masses.

<u>Untapped Energies</u>

All of us
can change lives
for the better.

The concept
of vividly picturing
in your mind
that change
releases great,
untapped
energies.

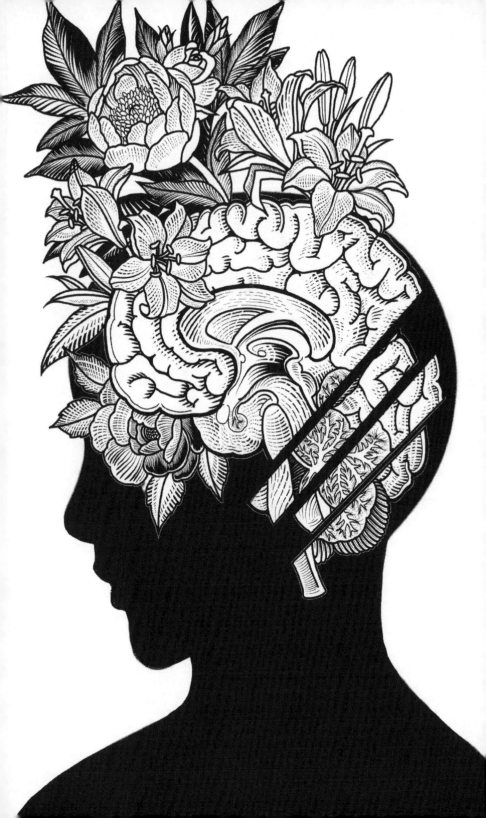

Confessions from a Broken Mind
(A Journey Through Introspection)

Confession One

"I have always attempted to perceive the beauty in the world in hopes that it would help me acquire an admiration for life. I suspected that's where true happiness would always blossom from."

Joy, for many individuals, manifests itself as the pleasures that stem from the simplicities life offers: the gentle sloshing of ocean waves colliding with a rocky shore, night-driving under the illumination of a vibrant full moon, casually reading in the cool shade of a sun-bathed park. As others dwell in the pursuit to rack up countless achievements and milestone-worthy successes, these remarkably lucky people find the true root of happiness through their ability to appreciate life in its simplest state.

I sincerely wish my own ability to perceive life in such a manner didn't feel so *diluted*.

Imagine the source of your happiness being noticeably weighed down by an anchor you cannot detach. Imagine experiencing a magnificent sight, something truly remarkable, through a valley of fog that suppresses the bulk of your emotions and diminishes what you could be feeling. You appreciate what's unfolding in front of you immensely, acknowledging the astonishing beauty of what your eyes are observing. However, you're also consciously aware that you're disconnected from your true self, a casualty to a darkening presence whose location you cannot pinpoint. This presence seems omnipresent by design.

That's not to say that I don't experience brief moments of clarity, instances where the fog momentarily thins and unhindered happiness rushes through me: The infectious joy produced from a child's smile; the affection received from a lovable animal; witnessing a heart-warming demonstration of humility, one that positively changes my perspective on life. These glimpses of pure happiness are instances forever embedded into my mind, remembered as vividly as the day they happened. I believe these specific moments of joy make life truly worth living.

Confession Two

"I have always longed to experience moments in life whose presence left a lasting impression on my soul. I always imagine them forever lingering within my mind as a reservoir of happiness that could be infinitely tapped into."

I already explained briefly that I've experienced glimpses of pure happiness in my life. I remember them so vividly because they left such a memorable impact on my state of mind. Unfortunately, these same memories cannot create the sort of feel-good reservoir I require to permanently eliminate what afflicts me.

It may sound strange, but I'm starting to become okay with that, and I'll explain why.

If you experience emptiness, sadness, and self-doubt so deeply that it nearly paralyzes your mind, you must also hold the capability to experience happiness as well.

Therefore, when my darkest hours occur, I try desperately to remind myself that this overwhelming flood of negative emotions will eventually drain. Deep down, however, I know they'll never completely empty.

That realization doesn't keep me from anticipating the moment the tides of despair disperse, and the depression subsides. For in those instances, when it finally does, I receive the chance to experience actual happiness. And when I do, these specific moments gracefully flow within the river of my memories.

These strands of memory are what I cling to whenever I perceive my mind drifting into yet another depressive cycle. They serve as a life raft, keeping me from submerging beneath the murky waters of despair.

These strands of memory serve as my lifeline.

Confession Three

"I have developed an awful habit of living my life in the past, reflecting too heavily on events or specific moments that only leave a negative impact on my perception of life. I replay these memories until it feels as if my mind will implode. Consequently, these actions force me to waste away the present."

Now don't get me wrong: I believe that reflecting on your past can be a healthy experience when it's performed to gain perspective on where your life is headed or to acknowledge how much progress you've already made. Unfortunately, whenever I dive into my strands of memories, I can truthfully say that positive reflection isn't happening most of the time.

As depressing as it sounds, memories that creep into my consciousness are usually moments that have been haunting the depths of my mind for years. Sometimes I reflect on tiny moments that affected me negatively, analyzing them extensively, but acknowledging how insignificant they are to my life at the same time. These are still memories that I dwell on, of course, but they will never possess the capability to eat away at me. Then there are the "mind-leeches," as I've begun to call them. These specific memories continue to consume me as the present passes me by.

Mind-leeches are negatively perceived life-changing moments that continue to selfishly devour both my mental energy and positivity. These memories tend to latch onto my mind, forcing me to overanalyze every miniscule detail of the events that transpired until I feel mentally exhausted. Heartbreak, loss, shattered dreams, and countless failures: these are the sort of moments continuously circulating, endlessly repeating within the confines of my head.

For some reason, I can't bring myself to let go of the past and embrace the life that stands before me. So consequently, these memories will only continue to linger. They will attempt to siphon the essence of life from me in relentless fashion and force me to desperately defend the prospect of my contentment. And I've grown to accept this in the loosest of terms.

Rest assured, hope still flows through my veins as thickly as blood. Even against the continuous bombardment of my most tragic memories, I won't quit fighting for possession of my life. I know I will find the strength to finally abandon the past that torments me. On that day, I'll reclaim full control over my future.

Confession Four

"The emotions accumulated from re-living my past help contribute to my self-destructive nature. Negative thoughts lead to negative actions, and those actions have destructive consequences. This is ultimately what ends up driving otherwise positive influences out of my life."

I spent three years' worth of hard-earned savings trying to purchase contentment concealed beneath a layer of nostalgia. I quit my stress-inducing job, spent every penny I had on my selfish pursuit of happiness, and ended up broke, lonely, and more depressed than ever before.

Admittedly, the concept of finding happiness by acquiring more materialistic possessions stemmed from me trying to fulfill my emotional impulses. Acquiring new possessions meant satisfying my desire for escapism, while simultaneously leaving behind a reality that was deteriorating before my eyes. It became an addiction fueled purely by a desire to return to a time of innocence and simplicity. A time where anxiety, depression, and insomnia weren't relentlessly wreaking havoc on my mind. A time where my dreams and aspirations weren't mercilessly shattered. And in the end, my self-destructive actions caused me to lose some of the most important people in my life.

Despite how this may read, this isn't some elaborate platform to spew my self-pity. I'm not writing this with hopes that you'll shed tears over my misfortune. Everyone endures the burdens that life can bring, and the concept of suffering is not mine alone to bear. I'm certainly not naïve to that. There's a significant reason why I've chosen to bare my soul to you.

With that said, we have reached my final confession ...

Confession Five

*"I've revealed my innermost thoughts and feelings to
you with hopes that my willingness to be vulnerable
inspires you to take a chance and do the same. Allow
someone you trust to peek inside your head, speak
to them about what burdens you, and find a source of
strength through these individuals. This war in our
minds was never meant to be fought alone. Seek
shelter in the knowledge that no matter how lonely
you may feel, you're never truly alone in this fight to
overcome what plagues you."*

The written journey that I've led you through was always
meant to serve a dual purpose. The first part involved me
searching for perspective through introspection—a self-
examination of my thoughts and emotions. The other,
significantly more important part was born out of the
hope that my unveiled confessions would inspire a change
of perspective within you.

Many individuals, including myself, were
ingrained with the misconception that concealing the
weight of their feelings represented emotional strength.
But that couldn't be further from the truth. Emotional
strength is overcoming what your mind perceived as
impossible. It's the sense of relief one receives from
surviving yet another soul-crushing cycle of depression.
It's the momentary silence of doubt-filled whispers and
the short-lived release of constricted thoughts. It's not
allowing your insecurities to crush your confidence.

Emotional strength means all of these things and
so much more.

Mustering up the courage to openly talk to
someone about what plagues you does not involve
sacrificing your emotional strength, nor should it ever feel

that way. It is increasing your strength. You should never feel ashamed of your willingness to be vulnerable to someone you trust.

With the purest sincerity, I hope my desire to share my deepest confessions with you gradually shifts your perspective in a manner which causes you to seek strength in others. I believe that is of vital importance, no matter how long it takes you to accomplish that. Understand that we are all facing our own internal battles, fighting with the ferocity of a thousand warriors to destroy what's threatening to consume our minds.

Some are just better at concealing it than others.

About the Author

Naturally gravitating towards writing since he was young, J.A. Handville found his true voice through poetry. Inspired by poets like Robert M. Drake, Neil Hilborn, and Donte Collins, J.A. Handville creates thought-provoking poems focused on the human condition, love loss, mental illness, and introspection. He possesses a sincere determination to help others overcome whatever burdens them and hopes he can achieve that through his work. J.A. Handville's poetry has been published in *Unvael,* and he anxiously anticipates his future publication in other established art and literary journals. He resides in Syracuse, New York, where the luxury of delicious pizza almost makes the cold, long winters bearable.